Binary Options:

A ONE – MINUTE PROFIT FORMULA

Alan Sedar

Copyright © 2014 Alan Sedar

All rights reserved.

ISBN-10: 1495295133

ISBN-13: 978-1495295133

DISCLAIMER

This book was developed as an educational tool only and should be reviewed with the greatest of care by its reader. The information in this book should not to be considered investment advice and is presented solely for information and educational purposes. Specific investments may not be suitable for all investors or readers. An investment in stocks, commodities, futures, FOREX, or other trading medium could result in the total loss of the investment including original principal. Anyone wishing to invest or speculate in any investment or market should seek their own financial or professional advice. No investor should attempt to invest more than they are prepared to lose. The author of this book is not an investment advisory service and cannot recommend the purchase or sale of any investment instrument. There are no licensed financial advisers working on behalf of this author. ANY REPRESENTATION OF HYPOTHETICAL PERFORMANCE RESULTS CAN VARY SUBSTANTIALLY FROM THOSE FOUND IN AN ACTUAL LIVE TRADE. NO REPRESENTATION IS BEING MADE THAT ANY ACCOUNT WILL OR IS LIKELY TO ACHIEVE PROFITS OR LOSSES SIMILAR TO THOSE SHOWN. THERE CAN BE SIZABLE DIFFERENCES BETWEEN HYPOTHETICAL PERFORMANCE RESULTS AND THE ACTUAL RESULTS SUBSEQUENTLY ACHIEVED BY ANY PARTICULAR TRADING SYSTEM. ONE OF THE LIMITATIONS OF HYPOTHETICAL PERFORMANCE RESULTS IS THAT THEY ARE OFTEN PREPARED WITH THE BENEFIT OF HINDSIGHT. THE RISK OF LOSS OF TRADING IN THE COMMODITIES OR OTHER MARKETS CAN BE SUBSTANTIAL. Trading is speculative and a substantial risk of loss exists. Past performance is not necessarily indicative of future results. This author cannot be held responsible for any resulting loss caused by the use and interpretation of information found in this book. The author provides no warranties, either expressed or implied, as to the ability to succeed in the various markets referred to in this book and shall be held harmless from any loss or other damages caused due to the reader's interpretation and use of the data provided herein.

Charts created using TradeStation. ©TradeStation Technologies, Inc. 2001-2013. All rights are reserved. No investment or trading advice, recommendation or opinions, are being given or intended.

CONTENTS

	Acknowledgments	v
1	Introduction	1
2	What Is A Binary Option?	4
3	Definitions	6
4	Introduction to Binary Options	10
5	Types of Binary Options Trades	14
6	Technical Indicators	16
7	Brief History Of Candlestick Charts	17
8	More On Technical Indicators	19
9	Key Indicators Used	20
10	Building the Platform	23
11	The Strategy	31
12	Cash Management	40
13	The Math	41
14	Selecting an Online Firm	45
15	Summary	47

ACKNOWLEDGMENTS

I would like to thank my wife and family for their patience and support during the countless hours I spent perfecting this process. I would also like to thank the folks at Interbank FX, LLC for allowing the use of images generated from their MT-4 Software Platform as a part of the studies presented in this book.

INTRODUCTION

People continually seek new ways to earn extra money. Many will start a small business. Unfortunately statistics show that at least 85% of new small businesses will fail in the first year. Many have tried to build their own website, find a group of products to sell, build a site, and then review all the advertising options that are available. With very little experience, people will measure website rankings, SEO key words, things they have little knowledge of. After spending months trying to improve their website ranking to get more traffic, they finally decide to pay a service to help. A few thousand dollars later they would eventually realize they are spending, not making money, and they will give up the venture in debt and with less money than they had before. The small business statistic holds true again and again.

Others will get talked into "blogging for dollars". Their hope is that the idea they are selling will take off. They will spend hours and hours trying to build "back-links" and improve their web rankings. Or they will consider social media advertising. Again, without expert knowledge, their efforts are doomed for failure. In an effort to keep costs down people will also consider a home-based business. Again, the startup costs, maintenance costs, and other expenses in this electronic age are such that it takes quite a bit of money just to get things started, and a skill set to match! And even that combination will not guarantee success.

So what is the answer? If we are looking for a way to make money without any of the heartache found in the above examples, don't want to sell to family and friends, don't want to make a huge investment into some idea that may not work, do not want to try and duplicate another's supposed success using their website, are not keen on network marketing, then what other choices does a person have?

BINARY OPTIONS: A 1-Minute Profit Formula

This manual was developed as a way to introduce people to a very low cost way to make extra money either part time, or with a little effort, build an income. A friend of mine said that to win at anything, you only have to be right 51% of the time. This plan could improve those odds significantly.

With Binary Options we don't have to sell anything to anyone, we don't have to bother family and friends, we can work this system at home or anywhere with access to a computer for that matter. In this manual, we will explain what a binary option is, show a strategy that could help the user understand this device and improve their odds to the point that 51% will look low. With a little applied study, it is quite possible to begin to make a little money almost immediately. And, over time, this process could help them build a nice nest egg. After all, we are in it to make money, not to spend it.

Binary Options were developed as a way to enter an investment market with very little money and with very little risk. The manual will go into more detail, but the author can say that after a very short learning period, a person could begin to make some potential gains without all the baggage associated with those other schemes mentioned before. Now don't get me wrong. Some people do make money in those venues, but I haven't met very many truly successful ones. With Binary Options, some platforms allow a person to start with as little as $100 to open an account.

The point of it is that we are introducing a system to help people make money from the privacy of their own home without having to sell anything, requires a very small investment, can be done at almost any time of the day or, with some platforms, into the evening or at night! If you want to work, you can make serious money on your own time at your own pace. Tired of those "highly leveraged" programs where you have to depend on others to help you succeed, then give this a try. You will be amazed how simple and economical this is.

This manual will attempt to cover such things as:

- Defining what binary options are
- A brief coverage of technical indicators
- How effective use of technical indicators can improve win ratios
- How candlestick charts can help one recognize trends
- A simple 60 second trading plan
- Money Management
- Begin to recognize changes in trends
- Using daily news to help make early day trading choices.

As brief as this manual is, its contents can quite possibly help the small investor take charge of their financial future and perhaps make some serious money. That is the primary objective of this manual,

To Make Money!

Take the time to review this manual carefully. You will find the income opportunities to be vast, continually available, and with the potential to build a very nice income stream.

We hope you will find our system profitable and wish you great success!

WHAT IS A BINARY OPTION?

This document will focus on a narrow band of investment instruments called "binary options." Unlike many other financial instruments, this type of investment is actually a comparatively simple way to make money.

A binary option provides a way to "bet" on the price direction or price range of a given underlying investment asset such as gold or silver. **Honestly, it is not that complicated**. The investment industry makes it tough on a new person who wants to make a profit. But with a binary option, one would watch a chart of, say, gold, and would purchase a contract often with as little as $10.00 taking a position that gold will go up from the price it is right now. Or one might think that the price of gold will go down. So the investor would purchase a contract saying that the price of gold will go down from its current price. If the person was correct in their analysis, they get back the $10 contract price PLUS a value of 70% of that purchase, or more! With this type of process, within as little as a minute of time, you could have made another $7.00 with a $10.00 trade!

For the purposes of this book, the above illustration summarizes what a binary option is, simply a contract where the firm will pay the investor a percentage over and above their investment if they were correct in choosing the direction or price range their investment moves for the time frame set in the contract.

To use the online trading platform provided by the brokerage firm by itself is not enough. The system being introduced will provide a guide and illustrations to help the novice and expert improve their chances of making money.

A word of advice: Take your time. Do *not* get frustrated. This may be a new concept to you, but after a very short time once the system is set up and the plan is in place, the investor will likely see that this is a very simple way to make money. The hardest thing to determine will be whether the price of the asset will go up or down in the time frame selected. This will become clear too.

Getting into the meat of this process, the author wants to give the reader a deeper background on the industries' use of certain definitions and how they will ultimately apply to Binary Options. It is not our intent to go into great detail on each concept, but merely to touch on these terms to help one see the similarities to definitions found with a conventional investment. This background should help both novice and more experienced person gain confidence in their activities. Rest assured that one does not have to be an experienced "trader" to successfully use the tools offered in this document. These terms simply help one understand the mechanics a little better. With understanding comes knowledge. With this system, even a little knowledge can be enough to make a fair amount of money. And that is what this manual is about.

If one chooses to enter this type of program without solid advice and training, and without a plan, then the end result could be a total loss of a deposit account. We don't want that to happen. Please review everything in this manual and apply those principals when taking a position in a trade.

DEFINITIONS

Before you read this section, understand that these terms apply to a huge industry. **Although the definitions may be applicable to Binary Options, trading in Binary Options is far easier than trading in traditional options like those discussed in this section.** The stock market alone includes an option to either purchase or sell a given stock. We refer to these as "buying a Call Option or buying a Put Option. The investor can also sell a "call option" or "put option". These same instruments apply to commodities, futures, and the world currency market, often called FOREX, short for the foreign exchange market. There are far too many rules involved in using traditional options.

In fact, there are so many options strategies available for trade that their review is beyond the scope of this publication. Just know that the term "option" is the basis for binary option trading, at least in name. The reader will learn that the differences between binary options and the standard types of options are vast.

The author does not want to go into too much detail discussing these other terms but does want to familiarize the reader with definitions of key terms that will likely be encountered on different trading sites. A Binary Option investor will most likely see the following terms used in their experience investing in binary options:

- Option
- Call
- Put
- Strike Price
- Expire
- In the Money
- Out of the Money

Let's review each term individually.

OPTION: an OPTION is merely a contract that gives an investor the right to either buy or sell an investment by purchasing that OPTION. The author could get into a complex explanation of options, but to keep the purpose of this program on track, we will limit our discussion to only those items that will help the investor understand the trading vehicles and to understand those terms, should they be exposed to them in their trading activities.

The CALL: When an investor purchases a "call", they are simply BUYING THE RIGHT to own a stock or some other investment once the price of that investment SETTLES AT A CERTAIN PRICE. Investors can also SELL a call. On every option trade, there is always a BUYER AND SELLER. To "sell a call" means that the investor will most likely have to give up the underlying asset if their counterpart exercises their CALL option, in other words, decide to take the stock for which they purchased the option contract. One may also SELL A CALL to earn profits on a stock that is already owned.

To summarize, a Call Option gives the investor the right to purchase an underlying investment once that investment reaches a certain pre-determined price, usually once the stock has gone up in price.

STRIKE PRICE: This is simply the price that an underlying investment must reach in order for the option to be exercised.

Purchasing a "CALL" option gives the investor the RIGHT to own the underlying investment If it reaches the strike price. The investor only loses the cost of the call if they guess wrong in the direction that stock will go. You see, a "CALL OPTION" is usually purchased if the investor believes the ASSET will go up in price OVER THE "STRIKE PRICE" OF the option. So if, for example, the investor wanted those shares of stock @ $50 a share but the stock was at $48.50. The investor would be gambling that the stock will increase in price over that STRIKE PRICE.

If the stock goes over the $50 range, the investor can "call" those shares and has an immediate profit in the share price if those shares are worth more than the $50 going forward. If the asset did not go over that strike price then all they lost was the cost of the "call option" or perhaps, $100.00. For some this gamble is worth it, because if the stock price goes down and they had invested $50 for 100 shares, they are locked into the stock at that price, or an investment of $5,000. Should the stock drop to $48.00 per share, they would have lost $200 already. This is calculated as their $5,000 - $4,800 = $200. By purchasing an option, the investor has limited their loss to the cost of the option and not the potential loss of a stock continuing to go lower in price. In this example, the loss was only $100.00 (Commissions not included in this example).

PUT: This is the opposite of a call option. The investor purchases the right to sell an investment at a given price. Some investors consider this a way to "hedge" their investment against an adverse move in the share price. An example would be like above, the investor bought the stock for $50 a share. They purchase a PUT option giving them a guarantee of selling that stock at, say, $48 per share. Should the stock go below $48 per share, then they have a contract that guarantees them the right to sell that stock at that price. This locks in their potential loss to only $200. If the stock continued to slide in price without a put option, they could potentially lose their entire investment. These options allow investors other ways to protect and fine tune their investment strategies to limit loss and maximize profits.

EXPIRE: All options are CONTRACTS, or agreements between two investors, one a buyer, and one a seller, of the option. Those contracts have a TIME LIMIT when they will expire.

We can get into a whole realm of investment strategies and theory, but for the purposes of this program it is enough to understand that each option has a TIME LIMIT or EXPIRATION date or time when the option is no longer valid. The investors then settle with payment.

IN-THE-MONEY: This means that the person who either bought or sold the option can exercise that option because it closed within the terms of their contract, or, was *in the money*.

OUT-OF-THE-MONEY: Obviously this means the investment was outside the limits of the contract terms so the investor lost their option cost on the investment.

Understand that investors use these vehicles for a variety of reasons. They are not always for the purposes of short term gains in the market, but can be used to protect an investment against a swing in the wrong direction or to afford an investor a way to purchase the potential to own something or enjoy the move of an investment without paying for the entire cost of the investment.

To summarize, the above terms are generalized explanations of investment terms found in a very broad investment industry.

Binary Options are far simpler to understand then the standard investments most people know as options. However, it was thought that the investor needed to have some exposure to these terms to gain a foundation from which to build when trading in Binary Options.

INTRODUCTION TO BINARY OPTIONS

The term *binary* was most recently used in the computer industry to indicate a numeric array extending 8 digits that indicates either an "on or off" condition of a computer command. With computers, a command, made of a binary number with its bits and bytes of information, was either on or off for that command. **With Binary Options, the trade is either "in-the-money" or "out-of-the-money", which is simply on, or off.** This means that the investor has essentially made a prediction that a certain stock, commodity, metal, or FOREX (foreign exchange currency) either went up or down from a given value at the time the investor placed his/her trade.

If the investor "bets" that the investment will go higher than the current value, (STRIKE PRICE) and stay there or moves above that number before expiration of the trading time, then the investment expires *"in-the-money."* If the value remains below that STRIKE PRICE, then their option is *"out-of-the-money"*. In common option trading, the name used for that value you are betting to be over or under is called a "strike price".

In short, one purchases a Binary Option "CALL" if they think the underlying investment will be higher than the current price when they first invest in that item.

In a more traditional investment, a bet that the value of the investment will go above the **strike price** is referred to as a CALL OPTION. This means that during the time period of the option, whether it is a minute, an hour, a day, or a month, if the price of the investment is found above that strike price at expiration, then the option closes in-the-money. If the price is below the strike price when it expires, then it is out-of-the-money. In the case of binary options, the term most often used instead of "strike price" is TARGET PRICE.

This value changes all the time as the asset price, or as some would call the asset the underlying investment, moves up and down. We will learn more about this as we look at trading strategies.

For now know that binary options have similarities to traditional options, but are unique investment tools that provide the potential to earn a significant profit often in a relatively short time period, and without the kind of risk associated with mainstream investment accounts or through other income opportunities.

PUT OPTIONS are the reverse of CALL OPTIONS. The investor is betting that the trade will end in a value BELOW the strike price, or price set at the time of the investment when the time allotted for the trade is finished. If the price closes below the *target price* when the trade time expires, the PUT OPTION closes in-the-money.

Some differences between binary options and standard options are- 1) the size of the trade; 2) the time the trade lasts; 3) the amount that can be lost during the trade; 4) the simplicity of a binary option transaction versus their counterpart in traditional markets; 5) Binary Options have no margin requirement; and 6) **the amount of money needed to start investing in binary options is very small compared to traditional investments.**

Traditional options command sizable underlying assets.

Traditional options are usually purchased on margin. That means that the investor will hold an approximate amount much less than the actual value of the underlying asset the option is based on in their account. As an example: An investor is not interested in receiving delivery of pork bellies. They are only interested in the value of the option over time based on the move of the market. Their margin account is then increased or decreased based on their trading success. However, the underlying asset could be significant. A currency asset could be worth $100,000 so any small move is significant and can affect an option price fast and with potentially devastating financial consequences.

Fortunately, we are not here to discuss traditional options. This section was given to help show the differences in cost and risk between traditional options and the binary option system.

In Binary Options, there is no such thing as a Margin Requirement!

Unlike a traditional option, **binary option trades can be placed for as little as $10.00. If the investor bets wrong, then $10 is the most they can lose on that trade.** Liken it to playing a hand of blackjack at a local casino. Win and you get your bet back and the winning percentage. **However, this trading vehicle can pay out in excess of 70% if the investor bets correctly and wins the trade.** I realize that $7 is not a great deal of money, but through continued trading on a routine basis, that gain can add up to a significant amount of money. Fortunately too the potential loss and the minimum deposit that a binary option trader must open an account with is very small. Some trading houses pay out as much as 85%. Now **that is significant**!

In truth, this trading vehicle provides the potential for someone to make significant profits in a very short time period.

So to summarize a few points:

- **Binary Options only RESEMBLE traditional options trading vehicles.** To begin trading in Binary Options, a prospective investor opens a binary option account, deposits a limited amount of money, and begins to make some trades.
- There is no margin requirement for binary options.
- There are therefore no margin calls associated with binary options. A trader simply places a trade with a nominal amount of money, and if they win in the direction of the trade, they receive the percentage payout in their account.

- If they were wrong in the direction of the trade, all that they can lose on that trade was the amount they placed in the trade to purchase their position, usually a call or a put.

Now let's look at some of the types of Binary Options Trades.

TYPES OF BINARY OPTIONS TRADES

One Touch: Your trade is based on the traditional assets mentioned before. The bet is that the price of the investment will either **touch** or **not touch** the **target price** of the **asset** in that particular trade in that moment. The opposite of the **touch** is therefore the **no touch** position.

High/Low: The investor considers whether the market will move above or below the target price of the asset selected for investment. Whether it is GOLD, SILVER, US/EURO, or some other option instrument, we have the opportunity to select the direction we believe the given trade will go and place our bet on that trade. Incidentally, this is the trade most often used in binary options.

Boundary: An investment based on the value of an asset falling either within a higher and lower range, or outside the range.

Short Term: This binary option has a very limited expiry time of 60 seconds, 2 minutes, or 5 minutes. Using the above or below option, the investor must choose whether to bet that the price of the asset will be above or below the target price at the time of the trade and that it will expire in the direction he/she has selected. As an example, Silver is trading at $23 per ounce. The investor believes Silver will end up above $23 during the next 60 seconds. The investor decides to place a $10 investment toward that position. If the asset closes above $23, then he/she wins the trade and takes both the $10 invested amount plus a 70% payout of an additional $7 replenishing his/her account up by $17. Net gain on this investment would be $7. Of course, the more money placed on the option, the more the potential win. But, a losing "bet" only takes down the account by the amount originally bet. The investor should institute a cash management approach to this investment.

DO NOT BE IN A RUSH. You will have plenty of time to make money. And if applied properly, you can make quite a lot of money too.

The author realizes that this might be foreign to the reader. And, it might not be what was expected. Don't be too concerned. Persevere. The system to be explained should make this process simple to follow and understand.

People routinely make bets at casinos or with lotteries with all but a very slight chance of winning. YOU PURCHASED THIS BOOK TO LEARN HOW TO "MAKE MORE MONEY." Our formula can help improve those odds drastically.

In the "introduction" we spoke of other income opportunities. However, the negatives of each include:
- *The amount of money required to start*
- *Significant risks associated with each opportunity*
- *High failure rate of each form of business*
- *Amount of time required for each*

Given that the results are so bad for most other income opportunities, one must consider Binary Options as a viable alternative. So do just that! Learn how to make money first, and then apply those skills to a lifetime of earning more and more.

Our strategy will certainly provide another tool you can use to meet those goals. So please stay with the author while this information leads to a trading strategy **anyone can use** with the potential to make MONEY.

The foundation of this trading strategy includes the use of certain market indicators that, when sampled together provide insight into the PRICE DIRECTION of a given trading asset.

TECHNICAL INDICATORS

There are virtually thousands of books of information on technical indicators one can select to help the investor make wise investment choices. Unfortunately, a person could lose a lot of money testing some of the more exotic indicators. The author feels that there are obvious indicators that are simply too intricate for the beginner to use effectively to make gains in a fast paced options market.

For the purposes of this strategy, the author will focus on the following technical indicators:

- Moving Average Convergence/Divergence (MACD)
- Commodity Channel Index (CCI)
- Money Flow Index (MFI)

We will keep this as simple as possible and still offer a background of each tool for the reader's benefit.

The author also prefers to use the "CANDLESTICK" chart. Other chart options include a standard close only graph and the "open/high/low/close indicator chart. The difference in using the candlestick chart is that it gives a better visual of the high and low and also gives a clearer sense of direction through the use of a colored candle. It is really a personal preference when an investor sets their chart parameters, but the candlestick method brings centuries of study and methodology to the art and science of commodity charting.

BRIEF HISTORY OF CANDLESTICK CHARTS

The candlestick charting method has been in use for centuries. The candlestick method was reportedly refined and used somewhere in the mid 1700's by a Japanese businessman name Munehisa Homma. Although option trading was rumored to have been in existence for a much longer period, it was Homma's continued tracking of the psychology of the market through the use of candlestick charting and the great wealth he reportedly gained through his use of this system that this method gained prominence in the commodities markets. And what were they trading back then? Rice contracts!

When using any investment strategy to interpret performance characteristics, one must know that, for every trade, there is a buyer AND a seller. And ultimately, there will be a winner and a loser to that trade. **The candlestick method was refined to help the investor interpret investor sentiment**. **The height of the candle, the length of the wick above, or below the candle, and the direction of the candle, meaning either going up in price or down in price, all help show the development of pricing patterns for that investment.** In fact, the candlestick method was further refined to include a width to the candle indicating volume. For most charting, however, this form of candlestick design is normally not found and is rarely used by most modern charting services or in those presented in trading software.

The selection of the candlestick chart design offers the reader another way to help interpret trends and trading patterns within a given investment. As investor sentiment wanes, a given pattern may become evident. To the alternative, as sentiment improves for a given investment another pattern may present itself that could help the investor more accurately predict the movement of the investment and therefore make the right decision in their trade.

In this chart, the "White" candle before the black candle with the red line through it has a wick above and a short wick below. The wick above the candle shows that the maximum price could not hold. The previous candle shows a bear candle with a wick at the bottom. It never regained its high from the previous trade. As we approach the bottom of the chart we see a character called a "Doji". This symbol is actually a candlestick that has a top wick, bottom wick, and its open and close are the same. It forms a "cross". It usually indicates uncertainty in the market direction. Be aware that there are both bull and bear Doji indicators so be careful trying to determine a price change on that information alone. Although we will not get into the great well of knowledge surrounding candlestick trading indicators, there is enough information given in this book to help guide one toward a proper solution. Now the investor will also notice that the three "trend" lines cross over with the short 3 period time accelerating lower. This confirms a negative trend. For 1-minute trades, it would be tricky to figure out the real direction so more time and a confirming indicator would be used to help determine what the trader should do next.

When we start studying the actual investment system, we will review a few key patterns one must be aware of along with other confirming technical indicators that should help the investor select the right position to take in a trade. But understand that a bullish candle is read as "open" at the bottom of the body of the candle, "high" at the top of the wick above the candle, "low at the very bottom of the lower wick of the candle, and "close" at the top of the candle body. A bearish price, or, one that closes lower than the previous closing price starts at the top of the candle body but then ends or closes at the bottom of the candle body.

Although this may sound difficult to understand at first, once the investor decides to try their hand at this form of investment, they will have already created the tools to make this simpler to see in actual practice.

MORE ON TECHNICAL INDICATORS

There are volumes written about the use of technical indicators to help determine the price direction of an investment. An investor most likely would go broke long before they could test all of the indicators and methods of analysis available for their use.

For now, focus on how the CCI and MFI indexes trend on each chart. Watch for narrowing trends in the candlesticks. Watch as the three MACD moving average lines begin to converge or meet at one point in the charts. A crossover could indicate a longer lasting change in trend that has developed which can result in nice gains to your account.

As this method is studied, we will be able to better interpret the data so as to make the right choice in an investment position to win the trade.

Through our examples provided within this book, the user will begin to see in far simpler terms, how this investment works, and will ultimately begin to enter trades that could make them a lot of money.

So let's first review a few of the technical analysis tools we have used in our illustrations.

KEY INDICATORS USED

The first tool is we will use in our charts is the MACD or, Moving Average Convergence/Divergence indicator.

This is *a real fancy name* for an indicator that is simply a colored line that shows the trend of an investment over a specified time period, on average.

To explain: if a 3 period and 5 period time is used and the time selected is minutes, then we would be viewing a change in price for both a 3 minute and 5 minute time frame averaged over a formulated time period, These price changes are averaged using a complex formula that is beyond the scope of our work. The formula is not important to us by itself. **What is important is to know that the two time periods usually cross as the price changes directions.**

For the purposes of this system, the author has selected to place not just two, but 3 MACD indicators in the chart. Levels have been set at 3, 5, and 15 in most cases. This was done to help the reader view movement close to the time price sentiment changes, or "crosses over" the existing pattern for the selected investment. As the two indicators cross, the price will most likely follow the direction of the shorter term indicator. If the 3-period is trending down and crosses over the 5-period, then there is a good chance pricing is headed downwards. The reverse is true if it crosses the 5-period increasing in price. Understand that short-term indicators can move swiftly so they are not the best to track for longer term trends, but are suitable for the short-term system we are presenting. The longer 15 period trend line could indicate an actual longer trend in development. As we learn more about the charting program, we will find that we can change the time period of the chart helping us see if a longer trend is in development. Although this book does not go into detail regarding that feature, know that looking at longer trends could make short term trades easier to see and more profitable.

This chart shows the three MACD indicator lines that follow the chart. Notice that the brown and green "fast" lines are closer together than the "slow" pink line? The author has found that it is good to have three lines to help the investor see not only the swift changes in their 1-minute trades, but the divergence/convergence found in the overall price direction of the investment, meaning how the price indicators spread apart as the price change accelerates.

The reader will also notice that the candlestick trend chart is colored with "UP" colored in WHITE solid candle outlined in black and the "DOWN" colored as a solid BLACK rectangle.

The three colored lines provide an easy way to visualize trends in the price movement of the investment.

CCI: Commodity Channel Index - This index is most often used to see if too many people have purchased a given investment or if too many have sold a given investment. The terms "overbought" and "oversold" are often heard when using this as a form of technical analysis. The indicator uses the current price relative to its average price over a given time frame. If it approaches its extreme levels higher than normal or lower than normal, the potential of a reversal in price direction could be imminent. It is recommended that horizontal lines be placed through the properties window at both 100 & -100 to show where the limits of a price direction would be reached.

MFI: Money Flow Index – This indicator measure both price and volume to help measure buying or selling pressures of a given investment. These pricing pressures are perceived as being at either their highest at 100 or at their lowest near Zero. At their highest the indicator offers insight into a potential reversal of the price trend in a given investment. The opposite is true at Zero. When the price indicator approaches Zero, there is a very good chance that the price with change and begin to go up again.

We recommend that a horizontal line be placed at both 80 and 20 through the properties window for this indicator.

Our use of these three different charting indicators is based on the combined story they tell on the potential price movement of a given investment. It is by combining them on one chart that we can begin to see hints of changes in price direction thus triggering an entry into a short term trade at the proper time.

The next section starts the long-awaited SYSTEM you have waited patiently to learn!

BUILDING THE PLATFORM
Setting up the System

Before we can start to make money, we must set up the tools to help the system work. We do this by taking the following steps:

First open a DEMO account at IBFX. You do this by going to the following Futures Website: http://www.ibfx.com/

Locate the "Platform" tab at about the middle of the 9 tabs to the left of the search window.

Place the mouse button over the MT4 location and another window will appear.

Download their trading platform: MT4. It is totally free and is a "real time" market trading account platform.

Follow the directions to install the software. Make sure you register. It is free. They do not sell any information about you and, you will never be contacted by phone for anything including a request to open a live trading account.

This software platform will help you follow most of the FOREX trades, commodities, and other potential investments.

Now you have a key ingredient for tracking your investments in real time.

Remember. This is a DEMO account. For our purposes, IBFX is NOT to be used as a trading vehicle in and of itself, but as a source of "real time" data as a DEMO account.

Other things IBFX can provide include:

- Up to date news and recaps from the previous day's trading activity
- Trading Calendar. This flags investment events that affect the numbers. It also tells if the news is of normal importance or HIGH importance.
- Daily Trading Edge website. Go here: http://dailyforextradingedge.com/ whether you intend to use the IBFX platform or go directly to this site, you will find a wealth of information to help you learn more about this form of investment vehicle and how to trade profitably.

Once you have set up your DEMO FOREX / FUTURES trading platform, take some time to learn about the investments that the MT-4 trading platform offers.

It may seem like there's a lot of information to digest. However, it is better to take a little time to get comfortable with the DEMO platform as well as the binary option platform once a real trading account for binary options is opened.

KNOW that the IBFX platform is based on real options trading and should be used only in the DEMO "non-funded" position to help the investor track and observe the pricing charts. Do not open a live account or deposit any money in this format. That is for more experienced traders that wish to delve into real commodities.

On the next page a chart from MT-4 has been set up to show how the screen can be split into 4 mini-charts. Although not illustrated, the platform also shows the types of trades on the left side, the tabbed investment charts that will be set up for easy access that line the bottom of the chart screen, and charting components that can help the investor better plan their research.

BINARY OPTIONS: A 1-Minute Profit Formula

When one chart is clicked, it will instantly maximize covering the other charts. Four different investments have been equally spaced on this screen so they can be followed to see if any of them are beginning to develop a trading pattern we can use within our program

One can line up about 10 tabs so open charts can be changed as needed. As you gain experience, you will narrow down to a few charts. You will begin to see patterns and timing within those charts that may repeat, like a trading range. This is good for your business because you can follow the trade both up and down making money in each direction of the price movement.

But for now, let's finish the Chart Set-up.

See the tabbed symbols. These are all charts that are set up for easy access. Just click on the tab and the selected chart will become a maximized screen.

SETTING UP INDICATORS:

Open your Interbank FX Trader 4 software, which is an online trading vehicle. A brief free registration process is required. After you are finished, please log into your DEMO account. If you can't get logged in, simply place your mouse on "file" in the top left corner of the site and

LEFT CLICK. This opens a drop down window that includes "open an account". Just follow those directions again and voila, a new DEMO account has been opened. So don't worry if you can't get logged in. After all, this is only a demo account, not a trading account. You are using the charting software to help you meet your financial goals through the system being presented in this book.

If you gain enough confidence, skill, and experience, you can always activate a live account. However, know that you can lose all of your initial investment and more.

Now we shall begin to set up the trading indicators that will follow the live charts we are using for our investments. Next, select INSERT and LEFT CLICK. This gives another drop down list. Hover over INDICATORS and another drop down appears to the right. Move the mouse pointer over TREND and yet another window appears. Please click on MOVING AVERAGE.

Your screen should have a window in the center of the graph shown below:

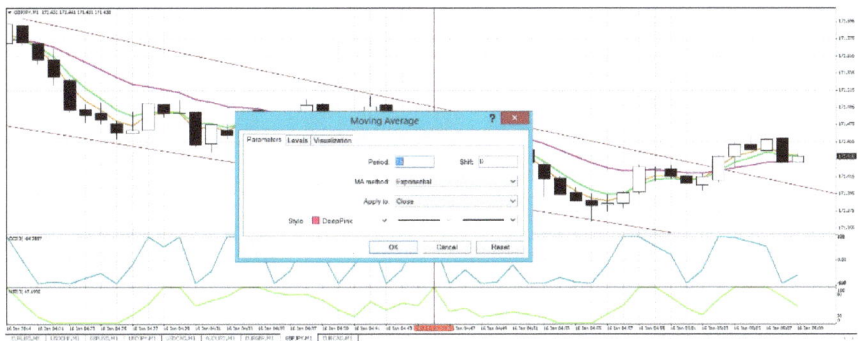

Our first indicator will be a moving average with a period of "3". Shift is set to "0".

MA method is "Exponential". Apply to "Close". Then select a color that can be easily seen on the chart.

You will duplicate these steps 2 more times, but will use a Period of "5", and then "15" for the third setting. Don't forget to select different colors for each indicator line, and keep them consistent so you can easily change charts.

When finished, the main body of your chart will include 3 different moving average lines: a 3 period, 5 period and 15 period line. The default price move is shown by a candlestick. Try to stay consistent with the colors and times so that as you move from chart to chart, the recognition of those key markers will be more immediate. As you become more adept at building useful charts, you will be able to take advantage of graphic options to help view changes in the chart more readily. The best advice to follow is always "keep it simple".

The typical moving average times are at 26 and 52 units in days. For the purpose of this system, **we are dealing with a time frame starting at just 60 seconds**, not in days or weeks, so the traditional time periods of 26 and 52 day moving averages won't help at all.

Once you have set up the above indicators on your chart, you should have a chart with 3 different colored lines woven between the candlesticks. For each new chart you wish to load onto your default window, you must duplicate these steps to assure that the information is the same for all windows.

At this point, your charts should have the default background interwoven within the candlestick pattern. We will now add the next two indicators that will show up as separate charts like those shown above in the same chart.

We will now insert one of the two key bottom graphs to the chart:

Select "INSERT" and a dropdown window will appear again. Hover over "INDICATORS" then "TREND" then SELECT "COMMODITY CHANNEL INDEX". That will place this indicator at the very bottom of the larger graph. Select a color for the line in the chart.

Follow the same steps as for the other bottom chart, but instead of selecting "TREND", go down two more to "VOLUMES" AND SELECT "MONEY FLOW INDEX".

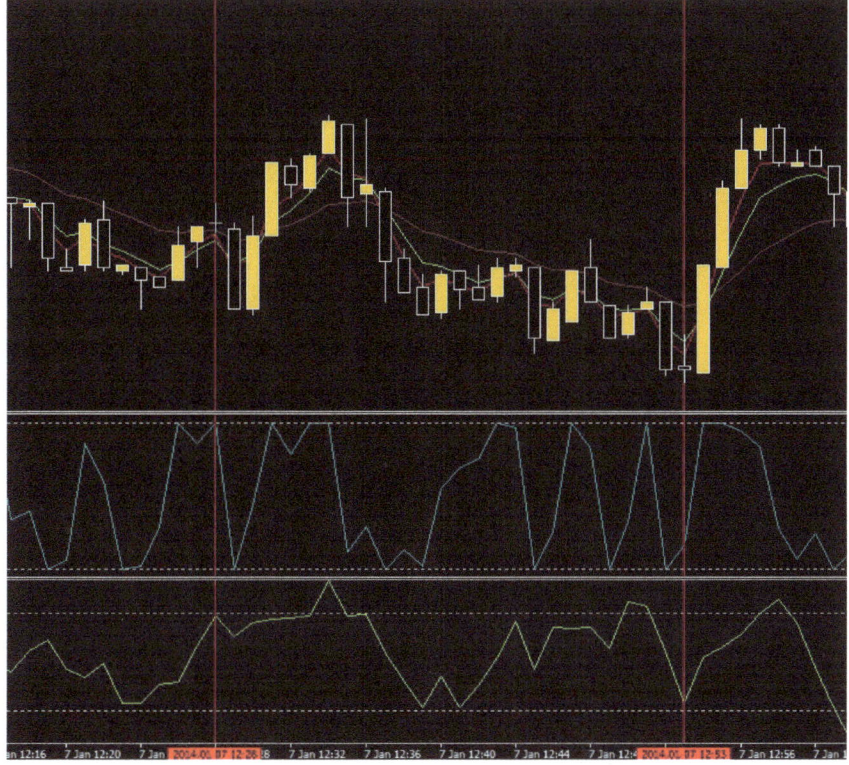

Once selected, the main chart will be completed. Each selected chart should look like the chart to the left. The commodity chart will now have 3 moving average lines of different colors, a CCI chart, and an MFI chart.

The Candlestick is a standard "default" view for each chart.

The red vertical lines were placed to show key price changes like those we desire before we make a trade.

As the reader gets involved in the strategy, or formula, as we would like to refer to this system, they will also notice on the chart above that the trends we discuss indicate a price movement down, a narrowing of price movement, a change in investor psychology, and a reversal of that price trend. Once this method is in place, the reader should go back to these examples to compare against their live charts. This may give insight into real profit opportunities. And as our goal is to make money regardless of the price direction, we want to make money trading both directions of the market.

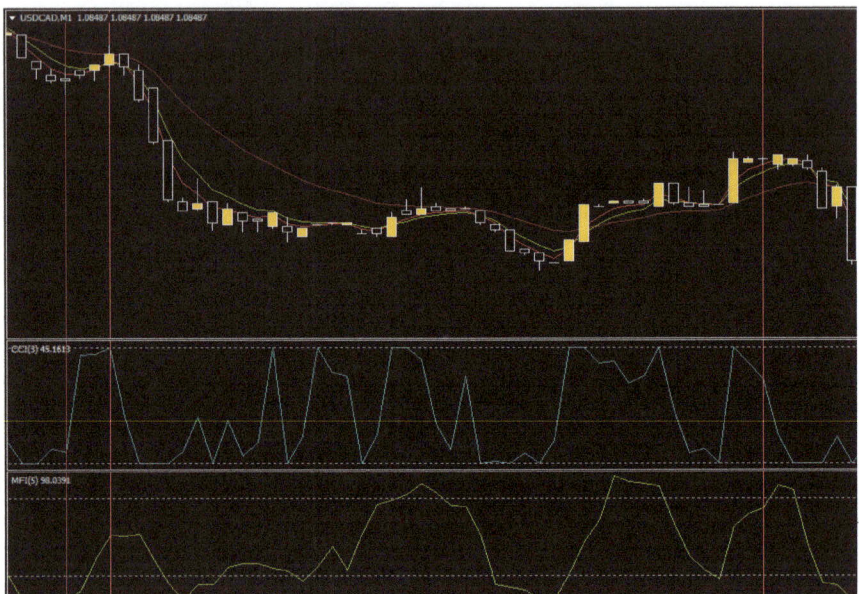

Once you do one or two of these charts, you will be able to move through any of the other available commodities, metals, or stocks that you wish to show on your trading platform and easily add those indicators. Remember to place the horizontal limit lines in the CCI and MFI indexes using the properties window for each indicator. You will find those options by right clicking on the indicator window.

The author recommends that you keep it simple at first.

Limit your charts to start. Become a specialist. As you study your brokerage demo account, you will begin to understand the system better and will also start to see trends that will help you spot trading opportunities to maximize your profits.

STRATEGY

The author has discovered a consistent chart appearance time and time again that gives a trigger point where one can trade with a higher level of certainty rather than just with a "gut feeling". In fact, this chart alignment has the ability to provide winning trades as high as 3 out of 4 times or better. This means that the user has the potential to win 75% or more of their trades using these indicators. For the purposes of this book, we will call this winning alignment "the formula". However," the formula" has nothing to do with math, but with following key trends and indicators that fall into alignment on the charts we just set up.

Take a look at the following chart:

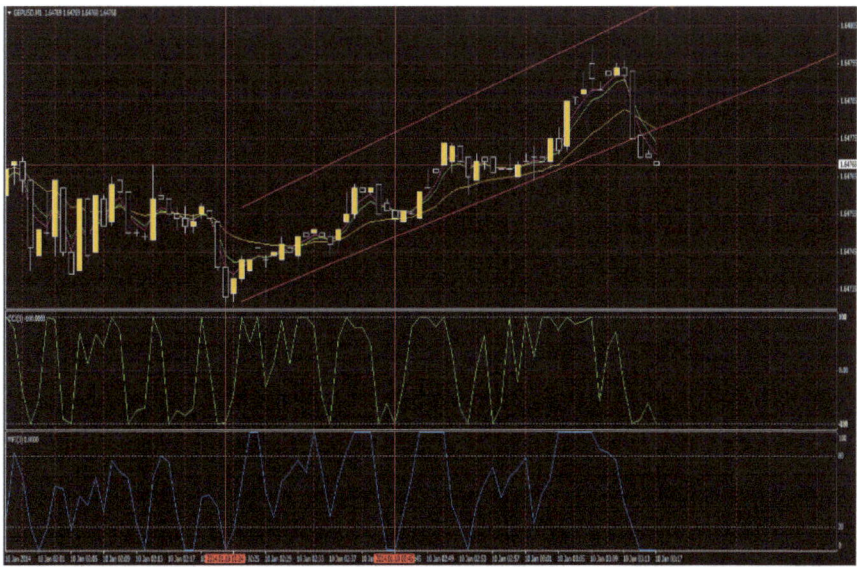

WE ARE FOLLOWING ONLY THE "ONE MINUTE" TRADE TIME using the Demo Charts.

Notice the vertical lines drawn through both of the bottom indicator windows and the candlestick chart? **Each bottom indicator either aligns at the top at or near 100 or at the bottom near -100 in the CCI index and above 80 approaching 100 and below 20 approaching 0 on the MFI index. Both indicators should be at or very close to the same spot at the same time for the pricing to be near a point of change.** You see, the Money Flow Indicator shows that money has either flowed into or out of the investment. When it also aligns with the CCI index, it shows a potential confirming position suggesting that it may be time for the price to change directions.

THIS IS VERY IMPORTANT!

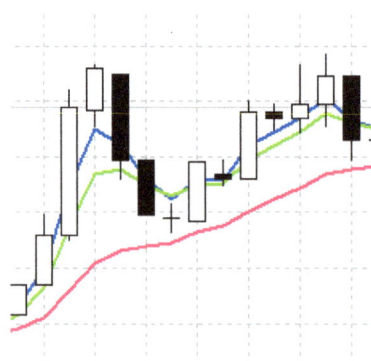

Now take a close look at the candlestick chart. When the candles get smaller, it means that the psychology of the traders is such that they are no longer as sure of the price moving in the given direction causing the open and closing price to narrow to a point of sometimes being the same. When a 'CROSS" is seen on the candlesticks, it is called a "DOJI", the ancient name for a candlestick where both beginning and closing values are the same. This is another confirming position that indicates a *potential* change in price direction. **This usually means that the psychology of the traders is such that they are not sure whether prices will go higher or lower, or that a change in direction is imminent. Use the other technical indicators to confirm the change in direction of the trade. We often say that the price has lost momentum.**

The reader should also be aware that a "DOJI" can present itself in more than one fashion as DOJI'S come in more shapes than a standard "PLUS SIGN". The most common ones are: the cross shown above; a bear DOJI, one with the wick at the top but no bottom wick; and a bull DOJI, where it looks more like a "T".

When studying the various charts, watch the trends to see these patterns develop. A combination of the three trend lines set over the CCI and MFI indexes provides a quality snapshot of time where pricing could change for a given commodity. In the next chart, red vertical lines have been included on the chart to indicate points on the chart where price sentiment has

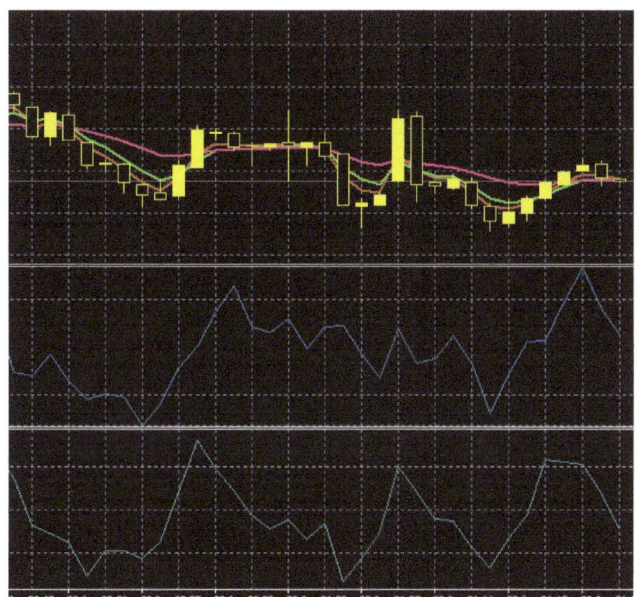

begun to change. The more "classical" the trading pattern is with the combination of indicators, the closer to a key change in price direction of the commodity. To maximize the potential win for your trade, the trade indicators below the candlestick, the CCI *and* the MFI, should be in alignment. Both should be at the top or at the bottom of the indicator chart box. To ADD, remember the 3 line indicators interwoven in the candlestick chart?

The two shorter time indicators (3 & 5) should be narrowing towards a convergence or should have already crossed with the "3-unit" line crossing the "5-unit" time period CONFIRMING a change in price direction. And it is good to continually learn and study the trend as this technique, like others, is not an exact science.

See the three MACD lines narrow?

See how the price candle narrows as a change in price direction develops? Also notice that the two indicators are at the bottom of their ranges in the two graphs below.

These are the signals we wait for when we choose to make a trade. And believe me, with a 60 second time for each trade, an investor does not usually have to wait too long for this type of signal to develop.

These types of signals will occur at the bottom of a price swing also.

In the chart below, all of the factors we discussed occur at the same time:

- A Gravestone DOJI (a bearish indicator) where the DOJI has a longer wick at the top and none at the bottom.
- The three MACD lines converge and cross over.
- The CCI is at or near its top.
- The MFI is also near its top.

Even though the MFI's change was tested, the other indicators were in alignment and confirmed the change in price. Also notice that the candlesticks were all lined up showing very narrow price changes. This shows that the market was uncertain of which direction the price of the investment would go.

When following charts, watch for these indicators described above as shown in the chart below. This trend is typical and has the potential to signal a real price change in an investment.

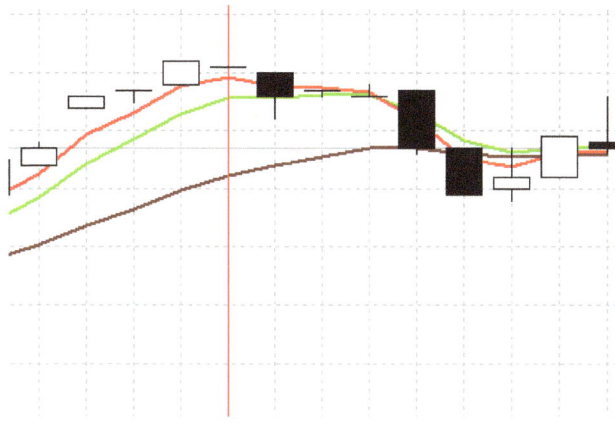 We try to track more than one trading chart to maximize our chances of finding this pattern on a given chart, but it is not necessary to do so. One chart can be followed at a time. Once the indicators are set to a given chart, they remain on the chart and offer Intel on how the price may move.

Review these charts and know that this is not a fluke found just in one commodity. The charting method works in practically all cases. On this chart, a DOJI appears just after a narrowing of a price move indicating potential changes in investor sentiment. Also notice that there is a confirming crossover of the MACD lines. Finally, see the step down in pricing. If followed with 1-minute trades, there were 4 good trades after the confirming down candlestick.

This is what we are looking for when we try to make money using this system.

See how the upswing in price has slowed and the MACD indicators have crossed. This shows a real change in pricing trends with the investment's price going lower. The vertical red lines were placed to show the point of change. By following the price trend, an investor could potentially make a half a day's wages in about 60 minutes based on a small investment per trade.

Note that the *CCI indicator offers similar trend analysis as that of* the MFI. In the chart directly above, see the indicators above 80 and below 20. The closer the MFI is to either 100 or 0, the more certain a change in price direction the commodity should be. Also see the narrowing of the candles when prices move in small steps. We will not always get a DOJI when price direction changes, so follow the MACD's along with the MFI. Pricing will trend in the direction of the MFI either up or down so trade with the trend.

ONE SHOULD ALWAYS RESPECT THE TREND.

DO NOT FIGHT THE TREND!

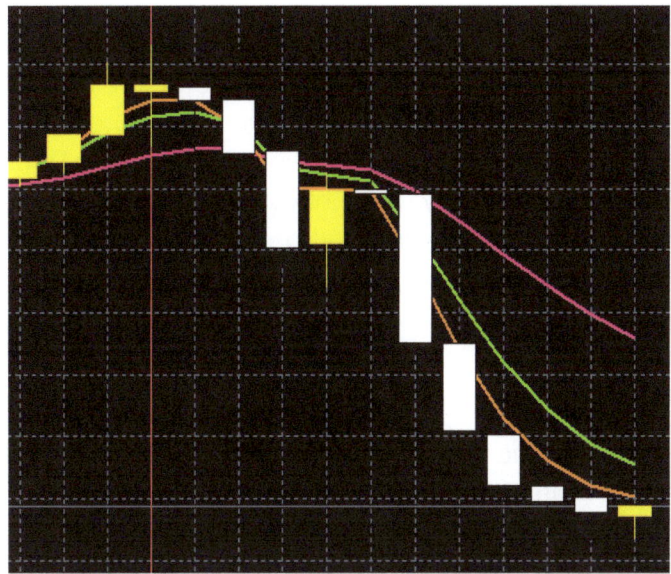

A red line was placed to show where the price momentum narrows just before a change in price direction, a key point to make a trade. **This graph is an exploded view highlighting the crossover and the narrowing candlestick in yellow.**

See that the DOJI is not always the point of change in price direction, and there are variations of the DOJI. However, the DOJI symbol is one of the easiest to spot in a graph that clearly indicates a pause or signals a point of uncertainty in the direction of the trade.

KEY POINT TO REMEMBER: We are looking for all indicators to happen at or very near the same time. The narrowing candle, the CCI close to 100 or -100, with the MFI above 80 or below 20 at the same time the CCI is at its high or low position, and at least two of the three MOVING AVERAGE lines at or near convergence (meeting or crossing at a point). An exact convergence does not always happen since we are looking at a 1-minute time frame. *The convergence of all three moving average lines usually means not just a short term move, but one that lasts for more than a minute or more.* As the longer time line breaks away from the two short-term lines, the greater the chance that a price trend has occurred that may last for a number of periods, or minutes. However, that does not mean we should get "reckless" in trading as short-term trades are intermittent and will not always move in a straight line.

Refer again to the chart on Page 36

From the top of the price trend to the lower price, there was an approximate 22 minutes of trading time. Of those minutes, 9 were clearly lower than the previous closing time period. And, of those that were closing higher, they were not confirmed with any change in signal meaning our signals did not confirm a real change in price direction. Both the CCI and MFI should remain at the bottom of their own graph indicating that money was still flowing OUT of that particular trade, meaning the investment was still being sold.

The convergence of the moving averages did not occur at the top, but their move confirmed a lower price as they crossed with the spread widening as the short time (3-minute) moved ever lower.

Trading into this trend would have built your account swiftly.

But be careful of unconfirmed short term moves. They will trick an investor into 'FORCING' a trade.

This trading method may also work with other time frames, but is has only been tested to confirm the analysis using a 1-Minute time frame.

And, when you have the potential to earn 70% or better per trade within a minute of time, why would you want to wait for a longer trading period to develop? The payout is usually no different, and too many things can happen during that extra time.

DOES THIS SOUND HARD? DOES THIS LOOK HARD?

IT REALLY ISN'T!

Key to success is building a chart using the "live" DEMO" account and using the broker's DEMO account together to begin tracking movement and getting comfortable betting on those trades.

Once charts are set up with the steps given above, **open a trading account through a trusted BINARY OPTIONS firm. Ask for it and you can expect to be provided with a BINARY OPTION _DEMO ACCOUNT_.** This is a free trading account used to practice without risk of loss. Use this to fine tune your skills.

A few trusted Binary Options Firms are listed under "SELECTING A FIRM".

DO NOT TRADE "LIVE" BEFORE YOU TEST YOUR CHART AND GET A FEEL FOR THE TRADING FORMULA. The best practices include viewing both Real Time Charts while viewing your new Brokerage Binary Options Account at the same time.

One can open both the DEMO IBFX trading account (to use for charting and tracking), as well as a free binary options DEMO account. The binary DEMO account trades with free token dollars.

After you have traded for a few days and only after you begin to make some money, TAKE THE PLUNGE. You can now consider going LIVE.

CASH MANAGEMENT

- EVERYONE'S RISK TOLERANCE TO LOSS IS DIFFERENT.
- DO NOT TRADE MORE THAN YOU CAN AFFORD TO LOSE!
- TAKE LITTLE STEPS AND GET COMFORTABLE USING THIS SYSTEM.
- BEGIN TRADING WITH A $10 OR $25 TRADE, THE MINIMUM TRADES ALLOWED BY SOME OF THE BINARY FIRMS. You will have to make a deposit before trading. But, the minimum for BINARY OPTIONS can be as little as $100, $200 or as much as $300 to fund the account. More can be invested. Consider that if it can be afforded because of the potential bonuses offered.

> It is recommended that $300 be used as a minimum deposit for a few reasons:

It provides enough cash to work with should there be a few mistakes.

That amount is usually the smallest amount eligible for a brokerage bonus. A larger amount could be considered and is not subject to loss by itself, but only the amount being invested in a given trade. The larger deposit often earns a larger bonus deposit amount. If you want your money back, simply apply for a withdrawal. Each options firm has their own policy on payouts AND how bonuses can be cashed out so review those points for your own benefit.

You will only be trading with perhaps $10 per trade in that LIVE account once established. As you gain experience and build your account, then you may wish to trade in larger dollar amounts. However, with a potential trade every 2 minutes or so, it won't take long for your account to grow into something worth the time to manage.

THE MATH:

A friend of mine once said that in order to be a winner in "things of chance" you only have to be right 51% of the time. Our aim was to improve those odds so the average guy or gal could work from any location with a computer and make money. Given a potential of earning 70% per trade or better, we have provided a small illustration to give some idea just how much money we could make in a month's time being diligent and with a little effort.

A scenario is given below that portrays the potential win over a day's time. Although this is only a scenario, the math shows just how lucrative this strategy could be over time -

Based on using a $10 per trade investment winning 3 out of 4 times, the average hour's winnings could be about $74. Doesn't sound like much, does it? However, this assumes ONE TRADE EVERY TWO MINUTES FOR 30 TRADES PER HOUR. And, carried for only 7 hours a day, one can potentially make over $500 in a given day. And THAT is only risking $10 a trade!

At that rate, one could conceivably make over $2,500 per week, risking $10 per trade.

THAT COULD TRANSLATE TO OVER $10,000 A MONTH!

The above example implies using a 70% return on each trade with only one trade every two minutes for a 7 hour day with a 75% win rate. Now honestly, trading for 7 hours straight can be a bit much, so learn your limits. And also realize that as your account grows, you always have the option to trade a larger sum per trade.

But please don't get *too* excited yet.

Trading is not an exact science. Nor does it work like clockwork. A trader can be expected to win some and possibly lose some.

The above example also assumes a person has the time to become a full time investor in binary options.

THE PURPOSE OF THIS TRADING SYSTEM IS TO HELP A PERSON IMPROVE THEIR CHANCES OF MAKING SOME REAL MONEY IN THE MARKET!

But it doesn't matter how disciplined a person is, they are eventually going to reach a point of doubt, or they will begin to second guess their better instincts or will falter in following their trading cues.

As a result, we have provided a few "rules" to help one preserve their MENTAL, EMOTIONAL, AND FINANCIAL conditions moving forward.

THOSE RULES ARE:

- DO NOT EVER, EVER, EVER, FORCE A TRADE! If the conditions are not right, then wait! Look for a confirming trend.
- LISTEN TO THE NEWS! Follow your commodity or investment. See what is going on in the world. Remember that all technical indicators are the DIRECT RESULT of a fundamental condition related to the asset. An example of a fundamental condition affecting an investment would be a cold snap hitting Florida thus affecting the price of citrus. Although this is not a trading vehicle in our system, it illustrates how news affects the price of something.
- DON'T GET ANXIOUS. IF THE INVESTMENT IS NOT PRODUCING, THEN BEGIN LOOKING AT ANOTHER TRADE FOR POTENTIAL.
- AVOID EMOTION. This will destroy profits faster than anything. Be methodical and follow your system.
- BE PREPARED TO WALK AWAY. Sometimes we need a break. Our emotions can cause us to over think and apply misguided interpretations to our trades. When we start losing more than our formula should allow, take a break!

- Don't allow a great previous day's session be wiped out because we allowed our emotions to get the better of us.
- No Panic Trading! If you have experienced more losses than expected, consider these rules and "step away" from the trading platform. The purpose of this formula is to provide an" intelligent" system that helps remove emotion so one can act logically and with a method.
- DON'T GET OVERCONFIDENT.
- FOLLOW THE SYSTEM. PROVE THE SYSTEM. DON'T DEVIATE UNLESS YOU HAVE AN IMPROVEMENT THAT WORKS.

If we intend to use this system to make money and want to go full time, then be willing to invest time learning more about our world and about our investments.

INVEST IN LEARNING. Become a student and see if you can learn a better way to trade or fine tune the system to make it a winner for you more consistently!

So, before we discuss who we will select as our key brokerage firm, let's summarize:

Watch your charts.

Make sure the bottom graphs are either BOTH above the horizontal limit of 80 for the MFI and 100 for the CCI chart or they are BOTH below the 20 and near the -100 horizontal meter lines.

Watch that the three MACD (moving average) lines are narrowing towards a convergence with the hope that a cross over will happen signaling a change. Also be aware that this is not an exact science! Trading trends can change swiftly so be aware of those changes and begin to trade into the trend. If you lose in one direction then try to confirm a directional change or continuance and trade into the trend.

See if the opening and closing value of the investment is trending toward a short candle with a small body. Other ways to view the charts to evaluate changes in trends is to change from a 1-minute to a

15-minute chart. This simply offers another view that can help the investor spot a potential change in trend for a longer period of time. This trend could be your friend if you spot it and can trade into it for a few minutes or even for a day.

If this was selected as a "small business" alternative, then give it the attention it deserves. Every small business experiences a few ups and downs, so don't be afraid to make the investment and apply a little risk to your new business.

SELECTING AN ONLINE FIRM

We have waited until very last to introduce ONLINE TRADING FIRMS so that a solid understanding of this process can be digested. We feel this time will truly pay off in better skills and knowledge that can only improve one's financial picture.

Now that we have a way to track our investment pricing in real time, **we must select an online brokerage firm**. After all, we can't start making money until we open an account.

The author sought only brokerage organizations that consistently ranked among the top when using their trading platforms, for brokerage support, low initial deposit, their opening bonuses, payout percentages and the way money is withdrawn from the account.

Not everyone sees things the same way. And, different people can interpret and visualize data and information differently. As a result, it would not be right to suggest one site only. So, I have listed TWO top rated Binary Options sites that can be tried and tested using nominal deposits to see which one works best for the reader. Once set up, begin your DEMO trading using this technique. This will give some practice watching the trading screen while the chart screen built earlier is viewed for key corrections.

Two Top Binary Organizations are listed below.

The first is Regal Options:

If you like what has been presented in this package, then please follow the link below if you choose to sign up with Regal:

http://bunitd.com/?b=11&id=107427

Regal presents the more traditional set up for its trading platform and is easy to understand and use.

The second has repeatedly been voted as one of the top rated sites for binary options trading and has just recently been approved for European trading. The firm is Cedar Finance.

Cedar Finance also shows a scrolling news section for up to the minute news. Its link is here:

http://bunitd.com/?b=8&id=107427&c=654

While using as little as $10 per trade and with cash management, risk can be minimized as one still takes part in the potential for up to an 81% return on your investment. Note that the percentage payout on any given instrument is based on that asset and type of trade. That means the payout could be different should a different trade time, position, or other item be selected.

These two organizations are top rated and are poised to offer the best in class in service and executions.

They have tremendous support and offer training and other benefits to their members.

SUMMARY

As a final re-cap, we have tried to bring the reader from a starting point where a Binary Option has been defined to your satisfaction. We have also explained some definitions, uses, and comparisons to other more traditional systems.

Additionally, a step by step process was included on how to set up your ability to view live charts which are critical to your success. These charts give the most up to the minute information affecting your pricing levels and direction.
A trading system has been identified that could potentially improve a trader's win rate to as high as 75%.

Technical indicators and trend analysis was covered along with a short review of the candlestick chart history and its use.

A real trading "formula" was presented where a person can improve their win rate and might actually be able to make some money.

We have listed two Top on-line Binary Option firms to help you get started with a high level of investor safety and support.

We hope you have found this information beneficial and wish you the best in luck in your endeavors.

Good luck, be careful in making choices, and -

REMEMBER THE DOJI!

www.ingramcontent.com/pod-product-compliance
Lightning Source LLC
Chambersburg PA
CBHW040918180526
45159CB00002BA/513